# The CALL
# The Answer
# The Experience

CATINA L. MACKLIN

# Table of Contents

# ACKNOWLEDGMENTS

There are so many who have helped me develop both professionally and personally encouraging me along the way to put my thoughts on paper and for that, I am grateful. Words cannot express my gratitude to Editor Katherine Guerrero for her professional advice and assistance in polishing this manuscript." I'd like to also thank Graphic Designer Josh Minor of Minor Design, Co. for creating a cover design that displays and represents the true substance of my work. Thanks to Feridon Terry Photography for outstanding work and always showing a high level of professionalism while supporting my vision.

I honor and acknowledge my parents Larry and Frances who raised me to be a responsible, accountable and driven woman who looks to God for true direction. For understanding my long nights at the computer, I'd like to thank my children, Tynia and Jaylen. They were constant reminders throughout this writing process, that my work was not in vain.

## Introduction

What is your purpose or calling in life? Do you find yourself lost, wondering what path is best to take? Do you need direction to help you hone in on your specific calling?

This book serves as a tool to help you grow a greater awareness. An intensive look inwards will help inspire, motivate and activate your innate gifts and talents. Through personal anecdotes, I hope to encompass what it means to better accept and understand ones' calling. With an increased awareness, passion and motivation, you will discover your true calling. You will be able pass on these lessons and share your story or experience with others who struggle with understanding what their calling and purpose is in life.

What are you waiting for? Turn the page and begin your journey!

I was a shy and small child growing up, but always had the courage to do things the average child may not have felt brave enough to do. My neighborhood was composed of family – my mother's parents had 13 children and most of them owned houses down the street. Years down the road, the state named the road we lived on after our family's last name.

My parents were married and had five children. I was the knee baby, which was known as the next to the youngest child. My father was a local gospel singer and an incredible guitar player. I remember listening to his group's music on our record player every Sunday morning as we prepared for church. It made me so excited to hear my father's voice on a record. I never dreamed that one day my children would be able to have that very same experience.

My mother was a radical Christian and for as long as I can remember, she professed Christ everywhere she went and still does today. When I say everywhere, I mean everywhere. Her witnessing occurred in church services, ball games, graduation ceremonies, funerals, weddings, birthday parties…you name it, it was and still is out of this world.

I remember her often taking us to church with her every night of the week. The consistent presence of church may have been the biggest impact of my life. We would go to church so much and stay so long that even during the summer, we played "church" at home. My sisters and I would get together and act out what we witnessed in church as an interesting game. It was probably one of the things we loved to do the most. One day, I closed my eyes and sang a song called "Yes Lord." When I opened my eyes, several of the neighborhood kids were staring at me in shock and at a loss of words. They told me I had been singing that song for a long time. Time had escaped me - I didn't even realize that I had been carrying on for so long.

As usual I had started to sing the song as a part of the game, but something incredible happened. It was as if my spirit had left my body for a few moments and I was lost in the words of the song. I truly believe to this day that this is the reason why I can't seem to sing much of anything without passion, energy, or even with a straight face. I must have only been seven or eight years old when this experience caused my life to take a turn.

My desire for others to hear me sing revolves around a constant effort to evoke the same feeling and passion I did on that day. From that day on, I realized there was something different about me. I wasn't special or unique. I simply had experienced the great feeling of a spiritual connection as a child. It was as if life had just begun.

I was very quiet in school and never open to sharing what I was thinking or feeling. If it wasn't for my some of my older cousins, I would have been bullied because I didn't look like the other girls. As a teenager, I desired to fit in. Looking back, I never would have fit in because of the calling I have in this life.

Did any of those words in the previous sentence stand out to you? If so, you too may be one of those who will never truly fit in because of your calling in life. Your purpose will not allow you to fit in at times. Not fitting in shouldn't be considered a burden, but rather a constant reminder of the trueness to our purpose.

It took me years to realize my life calling. Have I made some mistakes on the way trying to figure what my calling and true purpose was? Of course!

People would hear me sing and say, "Girl you are a preacher." I would think, why would they say that? They would say things like "You can't run from it." For a while, I thought they were right. I was invited to speak at a few churches but never felt truly comfortable preaching behind a pulpit or having the title "preacher." I continued to sing when invited but didn't preach in the church again.

## Speaking of Singing

I loved singing in the youth choir when I was a little girl. I remember the first time I had the chance to lead a song in the choir. I don't even remember feeling scared. Every chance I got, I sung with everything in me. While I sung, it was if I was in another world. A perfect world at that. Nothing else mattered. Singing has always been incredibly intimate to me. I've always felt as if I was connecting to a world much greater that this world when I let my voice be heard.

As I grew older, my sister and I began to sing duets together at churches when invited. We had a two-part harmony and were an awesome duo. Our family was filled with singers on both sides. We loved singing together and complemented each other well. She would always take the lower note and I would always take the higher note.

When I was 16, we entered a talent show and were upset when we didn't win. We felt that we had nailed the song and believed that the judging wasn't fair. The main judge of the contest was a popular and professional gospel singer who we had witnessed flirting with one of the other contestants prior to the start of the talent show. When it was time to announce the winner, the gospel singer chose the young lady that he was flirting with the entire time.

My sister and I were furious, and it was at that moment that I vowed never to enter a talent show contest again. Mostly, I lost respect for the gospel singer and was so bitter that I would change the radio station when I would hear his voice.

Immature, right?  It's hard to put into words how hurt I was. I loved singing so much and took a great chance to put myself in the spotlight.  It took me a few years to grow past the disappointment of losing.

As I reflect on this experience, I come to realize how important it is to understand how we can affect others with our actions whenever we are on any type of platform. In this situation, it was a professional gospel singer that impacted me as a teenager. Whether you are a singer, teacher, counselor, minister, motivational speaker, mentor or even a parent, others are impacted by your actions.  We must take our platform seriously enough to consider possible effects.

You may be wondering what or how I feel about that gospel singer today. Let's just say, I matured and no longer hold a grudge about that incidence. As an adult, I have encountered him again and not only enjoy his music but respect his artistry. I learned throughout my journey that we all have made decisions that may not have been the best or that others understand.  It took me some years of singing to discover that experiences such as losing this talent show taught me that our actions impact others regardless of our intentions. Perhaps he made his choice based on what he felt was deserved. Perhaps my sister and I needed to work harder at that time to perfect our performance.

There is always a lesson in every experience. About 10 years later I entered another talent show in my hometown called "Brunswick Idol" as a solo artist and won!

Who would have thought?

The difference in this talent show was that the audience had to cast their votes for who they felt should make it to the next round. All the other contestants were awesome. The competition lasted for a few weekends until the contestants were selected for the final round.

## The Call

At 25 years old, I had two children, a girl and a boy. While I enjoyed being a dependable, stay-at-home mother I desired more out of life. I enjoyed keeping our home clean, cooking great meals and nurturing my family, but something was missing.

At that point in my life, I felt inclined to pursue a career that would allow me to deal and surround myself with people. That revelation was ironic, given the shy nature of myself as a child. I was not sure then exactly what I wanted to pursue as far as education, so I enrolled in school to major in Business Administration. I loved school and could balance going to school, working part-time jobs and taking care of my children. Laziness has never been a characteristic of mine. I've always been a very determined and driven individual. This has worked both in and against my favor. This nature resulted in me always keeping my word, regardless if something was smart or unproductive. For years, I kept my word that I would never enter another talent show and missed several opportunities. When I finally opened my mind to trust and do something different, I entered and won.

Although I loved working part-time jobs such as substitute teaching, I wanted so much more out of life. I kept having this internal feeling that there was a greater work for me to do.

One day, I had sung as a soloist at an event for a woman who worked at a prison located in my community. I met her during her break to pick up the check. When I arrived at the prison to meet the young lady in the front entrance, a correctional officer recognized my name and mentioned that her son talked a lot about me at home. She added that he learned a lot from me.

She suggested that I apply for an open Case Manager Counselor position. At the time, my response was, "I'm not sure if working in a prison is for me." She said, "If you can work with teenagers, in the school setting, and especially with my son, there is no doubt that you can work here."

Inspired, I decided to fill out the application and was hired about three weeks later. I began to work as a Case Management Counselor and quickly learned how to complete the relevant paperwork. Case management was not a challenge for me – by this time I had earned my bachelors' degree in Business Administration. Although I had mastered and enjoyed the work as a Case Management Counselor, I still felt as if there was greater work for me to do. I was not yet fully satisfied.

One day, a Case Management Counselor who taught a class about breaking the barriers that keep us from achieving our potential offered me the opportunity to observe her facilitate a group session. Facilitating a group is essentially acting a guide to the way people think and process thoughts. It was that experience that made another great impact on my life. At that moment, I knew exactly what I would like to do. I wanted to facilitate groups.

I was bored with paperwork, completing annual assessments and evaluations. I felt alive watching her group session – I knew then that facilitating groups was going to be my next professional move. I went directly to the Program Manager and made my request. She granted it immediately. I learned so many techniques facilitating group and used every challenge as a personal and professional learning experience.

Truly, my calling had to be attached to facilitating. I witnessed men's lives change before my eyes. I remember one of my group participants deciding that he wanted to make a change in his life to the point that he wanted to leave his gang. Having gang members as participants was not out of the norm for me. There were several times when I would have a group of participants that consisted of rival gang members. During group, they learned to get along with each other enough to receive the knowledge and skills needed to increase their ability to be more productive and social beings.

One day I received the news that one of the participants who had completed one of my classes had been beaten very badly. It was the gang member who had chosen to get out of the gang. Being beat up was one way that he would be able to be excused from being a member of this gang.

Per recommendation of the warden, I went to visit him and see exactly what happened. He told me that he had let the gang members know that he had changed his mind about being in the gang. He wanted to change his life for the better. To do so, he would have to remove himself from any negative or unhealthy influences. While he was in physical pain, he still felt that he had made the right decision.

How often in our lives do we make decisions for the better knowing that we will experience pain?

When we want change, we must consider the pros and cons. If the pros outweigh the cons, we decide to go for it. This man is an example of considering the long-term effects, regardless of short-term consequences.

While working in the prison, I continued to perform as a gospel artist on the weekends and met many great musicians along the way. Invitations began to flow, from requests to sing at church functions, to weddings to funerals. With so many performances, I thought it would be ideal to recruit a team of background singers to round out my performance. My sister was the first person I called, then two women I knew from church joined the team.

I was not singing as a soloist anymore, so we named the group to "Catina Macklin and Nu Vision." While singing, I would meet people who would tell me how much our singing impacted them. The positive feedback encouraged us to share our gift with people from all over the country. Naturally, the next steps were to record music and write. At the time, I wrote what was in my heart. Just before "Catina Macklin and Nu Vision" came to be, my father passed away from a heart attack. He had performed at a gospel event and was reportedly not feeling well. Those watching him let us know that he began to sweat profusely as he sang. They told my family that everyone thought he was just pushing too hard as he sung as if something had taken over him. He didn't want to go to the hospital and just wanted to go home and rest. He never woke up.

To commemorate my first year singing as "Catina Macklin and Nu Vision", we celebrated at the very place my father last sung. The building was packed with friends and family who enjoyed our singing. That building became a center for celebration until it become overcrowded.

In the end, I wanted to hold on to the memory of his last performance. I have often wondered what he would say or how he would feel if he was still living to see that one of his children had formed a gospel-singing group and was finding success and support.

Would he be proud? I'm sure he would have. I am also sure that he would have never guessed I'd be singing quartet gospel, which was his style of music. When growing up, we knew he loved quartet music, but we grew up in a church that explored a wide variety of music styles.

Singing and facilitating groups is a huge part of my calling. Was my calling to sing, counsel, manage a business, preach, nurture or act as a care taker?

I had to internally examine my life and do a little research before being sure of what my calling and purpose in life was. When I think about my low self-esteem and feeling small as a child, I believe that it is all because of my calling and purpose. When I think of the mistakes that I've made in life and even when I think of how I struggled growing up, I believe it was all because of my calling and purpose.,

So - what is my calling?

If I had a different path with different experiences, would my purpose be different? It is my opinion that every experience, every failure, every closed door, every missed opportunity, disappointment, and every situation that provoked me to do something different drove me to find my life calling.

In 2013, I started to wake up dizzy every morning. The room would be spinning, and the doctor diagnosed me with vertigo. About a year later the dizziness returned and was so dire that I found it hard to function at work and love my work as a counselor. After two years of suffering with the dizziness, I would no longer accept vertigo as my issue and convinced my doctor to refer me to a specialist. After a few visits to the specialists, I was advised that the dizziness was caused by allergies. However, I knew something was still not right. Finally, I convinced the specialist to order me an MRI.  After blood work, hearing tests and vision tests, he scheduled me for my first MRI.

I will never forget the follow-up phone call from the doctor. He told me that while I had a small arachnoid cyst on my brain it was benign. However, the location of the cyst was unusual, and I was referred again to another specialist.

I still live with the cyst today. I've learned to cope with it because of its small size. The doctor said while it would always be present, it was not dangerous to my health. For years now, I have learned to deal with spells of dizziness using self-talk and meditation rather than traditional medication. This cyst has required me to pay close attention to my feelings and thoughts so that I can live in peace.

The discovery of the cyst was another life-changing event. I began to approach my health seriously and assess the different ways I could provide myself with a good quality of life.

You may be wondering what the discovery of the arachnoid cyst has do with the calling in my life. The discovery of the cyst caused me to realize how short life can be. Every minute we have here on this earth is valuable. Every second, every minute, every hour, day, month and year counts.

So, I began to have a broader perspective. My awareness grew. My dreams began to become elaborate, to the point where I pondered them for days.

**Introducing Awareness, Visions & Dreams**

Many times, in my life, I sought to directly hear from God. I started to ask God to speak to me in my morning meditation devotional prayers. What motivated me to seek God's voice started with a dream of a woman in the grocery store. Someone had taken my basket full of groceries when I was not looking. In the dream, I became worried and frustrated, eventually having the store manager look through the security camera footage. The camera showed a woman take my groceries – I desperately began to locate her. My daughter then said to me, "It's not like your purse was in the basket, you can just refill your basket again from the shelves."

I awoke from this dream wondering what the message was. Was God trying to warn me of something? What was I supposed to do? After a few days, I still couldn't shake the dream. I shared it with a couple of people to try to make sense of it.

Two days later, I learned that the lady who had taken my basket passed on the same night I had the dream. I learned this from one of the people I shared the dream with who had heard the obituary on the radio. Shocked, I confirmed with the funeral home.

What was God trying to say to me?

I had no connection to this woman yet knew her name from my dream. The following night, I had another dream. This time I was driving. A full name appeared to me in black letters across the sky. In this dream, I was following a woman to her doctor's appointment. I woke up a nervous wreck convinced that this woman must have been dying. Luckily, I never heard news of this woman. However, I did hear that a woman with the same name went to the emergency room the same night I had the dream. The doctors could not believe she had survived the trip to the hospital.

You see, I've always had visions in my sleep. My tendency to dream is one of the reasons why I named my gospel group Nu Vision. However, I could never interpret the message from the dreams. After having such vivid dreams, my desire to seek

God for wisdom was urgent. Suddenly, the key to my life's success revolved around understanding what God was saying to me.

This moment of realization was the beginning of a new and fresh awareness. While we may be gifted with so much, we can only operate fully in our gifts if we actively seek direction and the voice of God.

## The Answer

After dreams that seem like visions, I am prompted to pray and meditate. Dreams were one way I learned to discover what my calling and purpose was in life.

I believe my calling is to be an intercessor and my answer to the call is YES!

My answer is to intervene on the behalf of others. When looking inwards at your own calling, there is no need to think too deeply. Look at it this way – when I am singing, I am operating as an intercessor.

When I am facilitating group, I am operating as an intercessor. When I am training and teaching others in any capacity, being a catalyst for change, I am operating as an intercessor. When I am speaking at events, I am operating as an intercessor.

I discovered that all the gifts and talents I have are best used to intercede for others.  That is the message I believe God has been trying to get to me. I have realized that I must continue to seek God in everything I do, including my work as a counselor.

## The Experience

Facilitating is a great joy of mine. Through my work, I've taken away some lessons I think can be applied in multiple situations. I've pulled some of the most meaningful lessons to share with my readers.

Some of what I share in this book reflects actual encounters I have had while servicing offender clients.

Some of what I share reflects how I have personally applied my experiences to developing as an intercessor.

Feel free to journal and take notes of your thoughts after reading about some of my experiences and reflections. Active journaling encourages in-depth analysis of the self.

During a session, a substance abuse addict in recovery stated that she did not think that she should have to stay away from substance abusers to reduce the risk of relapse. Turns out, her friends and loved ones were the ones abusing.

She felt that it was not fair to her loved ones that she not hang out with them sometimes. This was alarming to me, so to help brighten her awareness and provide a different perspective, I changed the question. Instead, I asked her what she would do if instead of substance abuse, the issue was being diagnosed with a contagious disease. In this scenario, some friends and family had a disease that would cause her to die if she spent time with them. The addict responded, "I'd stay away from them because it would be too risky for my health."

Because of our distinct paths, there are some things we cannot do. Once with are faced with a difficult situation, we must think differently and even change how we interact with certain people, places and things.

# Notes

_____

_____

_____

_____

_____

_____

_____

_____

_____

_____

_____

_____

_____

_____

_____

## Coming Out of The Fire!

There is a sentiment that God will bring you out of the fire and you won't smell like smoke. God spoke to me late in 2017 reminding me that there are times when our pathway is off-course. Sometimes we find ourselves going through situations that we never could have imagined. Some call these paths tests, some call them offsets and some even call them trials and tribulations. On the 12th of December 2017, I pictured these types of situations as a fiery furnace.

How do you come out of the fire without others noticing what you have been through? I often say to my offender clients in prison that it is possible to change so much that no one would ever guess that you have been incarcerated when you come out. It is possible to recover with such strength that when people look at you, they wouldn't dare know your story or what you have been through.

Let's look at fires.

What starts a fire? Fires tend to start by people being careless. Most are caused by smoking, recreation, or equipment. Natural fires cause large burn scars and take time to heal.

What puts out fires?

All fires are not created equal and what works to extinguish one type of fire can sometimes fan the flames of another and cause the fire to grow.

As I began to think more about this metaphor, I examined how everyone has their own struggles and ways of looking at things.

Some things we must deal with are seemingly handed down to us. We may reach the point where we feel so bad about our choice that we develop an unhealthy shame.

We can come out of the fire and not even look burnt. What we must know is what type of fire we are in and acknowledge how we got in the fire. We must look at the part we played in starting or fanning the flames. That recognition will free us. At some point, we must fight to come out alive without being consumed. This will require us to be humble enough to take accountability for our actions and act brave enough to make amends. While writing this book, I had a small kitchen fire. Although the fire was small, the damage from the smoke required that we stay temporarily in a hotel. Sometimes we go through things that puts us in a different position, but we must remember that it is only temporary. We must have the mindset that once things are clean, we can then "move-in". Cleaning is a process and patience and cooperation is key.

Notes

_____

_____

_____

_____

_____

_____

_____

_____

_____

_____

_____

_____

_____

_____

## Kool-Aid Story

Years ago, I was facilitating the first session of a treatment program with about 14 male participants. A few of the men said that they just wanted to get the program over with. To them, the program was a means to receive their certificate of completion. I let them know that I respected their honesty and that if they complied, participated and completed assignments given, they would receive a certificate, but it would just be a certificate. There would be no heart or substance behind the piece of paper.

As a facilitator, I learned the difference in content versus process. You get out of something what you put into it. I came up with this analogy about mixing Kool-Aid. You need all the ingredients to make good tasting Kool-Aid. When people want to skip some ingredients, and expect great tasting Kool-Aid, they say things like, 'I do not need to hear that part,' or 'it doesn't apply to me.'

But how can that be so if knowledge is power?

Some may settle for sugar water, claiming it doesn't taste that bad. Perhaps, some may have gotten used to drinking sugar water, because that's all they had. Sometimes it's harder to experience the fullness out of life, because it is something we have become accustomed to living without. Some get all ingredients required to make good tasting Kool-Aid but never stir it up.

Older people used to say you must stir up your gift. Stirring it up requires that you do more work. We get lazy and expect things to just happen.

*"Faith without works is dead (James 2:17)"*

# Notes

_____

_____

_____

_____

_____

_____

_____

_____

_____

_____

_____

_____

_____

_____

# An Ugly Sweater vs. a Gown of Humility

I recall a session that I had with a client who was upset because one of her peers had made her aware of inappropriate behaviors she had recently displayed. During our session, the client felt that her peer was just looking for a reason get her in trouble. During her recovery, no one had directly confronted her. This lack of communication and compassion must have evoked anger and frustration in her.

I began to share with her a story I created about a woman who was wearing an ugly sweater. No one felt brave enough to tell her that her sweater was ugly, so she continued to parade around in her sweater until someone told her it was ugly. I pointed out to the client that sometimes things are brought to our awareness in a way that hurts our feelings. In those situations, we can take the opportunity to examine ourselves and grow in humility. What if she were to trade in her ugly sweater for a beautiful gown (humility) and looked for opportunities to become better after receiving the awareness from someone else? Beautiful is the gown of humility.

# Notes

_____

_____

_____

_____

_____

_____

_____

_____

_____

_____

_____

_____

_____

_____

## Understanding the How and Why

I love those moments when I can help others understand change. It is imperative that we understand both the how and the why. Understanding how to do something is necessary to accomplish it. Knowing the 'why' helps add substance to the 'how.'

The 'how' is an empty cup and the 'why' is the liquid. We need the empty cup to pour in the liquid. Without the liquid, we just have an empty cup. Many of us may know how to do something and do it well, but if we don't know why we do what we do, then there is chance our work is in vain. The work is then superficial and easily replicated. There is a passion that comes with the 'why.' When we truly understand the purpose of something, we give it more! We put more thought and consideration in the 'how.' Our work then becomes so much more rewarding and we become innovative and proactive instead of reactive in our thinking.

In early 2016, I began to think - what if my cup is dirty or what's in my cup is dirty?

What we have experienced in life can cause some stains in our cups. We may have been hurt and disappointed so much by an individual to the point that our judgment is cloudy. We form our opinions and there is somewhat of a wall that is placed as a result. However, it is fair to say that if someone were to pour into us, we could still possible enjoy to some degree the liquid in our cups. These stains in our cups can wash away.

One night, I was watching a reality show where a woman asked another what her favorite foods were. She then asked what the other woman would do if the meal was prepared but then served on the top of a garbage can lid instead of a plate. The woman responded that she would not eat the food.

What does this have to do with the stained cup? One may be turned off to drinking a substance from a stained cup. Although you may have been through some things that resulted in hurt or disappointment, we must act kind so others won't miss the true substance of who we are.

Notes

_____

_____

_____

_____

_____

_____

_____

_____

_____

_____

_____

_____

_____

_____

_____

## You Are What You Believe

When you believe in something so much, it becomes a part of who you are. It is your very being. Thus, when people enter your presence or your place of dwelling, they should feel that part of you automatically. You are what you believe! Imagine what an atmosphere would be like if there were at least two or more who shared the same belief in one room together. Now imagine what the atmosphere would be like if there were hundreds of people sharing the same belief in one room together. What would the atmosphere of a room full of people like you be like?

# Notes

_____

_____

_____

_____

_____

_____

_____

_____

_____

_____

_____

_____

_____

_____

## Jealousy

Jealousy can cause conflict to the point that we get distracted and off-track of our path. Jealousy can cause us to lose focus and forget the big picture. As a woman, I had to learn not to allow the spirit of jealousy to distract me. I had to learn to celebrate others' accomplishments. Too often, we focus on the success of others to the point that we lose sight of who we are, our gifts, what make us special and unique. Our thoughts and energy is instead focused on the gifts and unique characteristics of others. That is no way to live.

I recall a story about a man who had hired a group of men to do work for him. They agreed that they would receive the pay of one penny a day. The man hired other men who needed a job later in the day. At the end of the day, he paid all the men a penny. Some of the men who had worked longer hours began to complain because they felt it was not fair that they had worked longer hours and in the heat of the day and they all received the same pay. The employer replied, did you not agree to work for a penny a day? Have I done anything wrong? Is it right for you to be upset with me because I have a good heart and kept my word? The employer ended saying "One day, the last shall be first and the first shall be last, for many are called, but few are chosen."

My prayer when I present at a meeting or conference or sing on stage where others too have performed is that I remember the bigger picture. What is the purpose and vision of why I am doing the work I do in the first place? I pray for humility and strength.

What good is it to be great at something but not be devoted to the purpose? It would be like preparing a beautiful meal that no one can consume because of toxic ingredients. What benefit is there to have prepared a big feast that looks and smells delicious but is inedible because it's toxic?

Jealousy is just that - toxic! It sometimes motivates people to work harder at something just so that they can outdo or compete with others. What reward is there in the end? The spirit of jealously is toxic. It is superficial.

# Notes

_____

_____

_____

_____

_____

_____

_____

_____

_____

_____

_____

_____

_____

_____

_____

## Look Again!

Sometimes we fail to take a second look at a situation because our negative thinking has blocked our minds from seeing clearly. Sometimes what seems to be bad news is not bad news. However, the way we look at it causes us to receive it badly. If we take a second look, we may see that what we need is not so far away.

I recall the story of a blind man who met someone who could heal blindness. The healer took the blind man by the hand and led him out of the village. He then spat in his eyes, laid his hands on him and asked, "Do you see anything?" The blind man replied, "I see people, but they look like trees, walking." Then the healer laid his hands on his eyes again. When the man opened his eyes again, his sight was restored, and he saw everything clearly.

# Notes

_____

_____

_____

_____

_____

_____

_____

_____

_____

_____

_____

_____

_____

_____

## Reach Out

On Christmas morning in 2017, I was sitting in an early morning church service when I heard a woman speak about how Jesus could heal and deliver without ever going to medical school. She stated that while he never went to medical school, he was the greatest healer. He could give sight to the blind, speech to the mute and the ability to walk for those who could not. He was so powerful that he could even bring a dead person back to life.

She brought up the story of a woman in the bible who had issues with blood for twelve years. One day, she heard that a man who was such an amazing healer was passing through. She said to herself, "If I could just touch the hem of this man's garment, I'll be healed and made whole again." When Jesus walked through the crowd, the woman pressed her way to the front and reached to touch a cloak hanging from his garment. Jesus turned around and asked, "Who was it that touched me?"

As I sat in church and listened to this woman tell this story, particularly how amazingly powerful this man was and still is even after being crucified, I thought about how so many people wish to be touched by him. They wish and long to feel his presence. People often speak about how they long to experience the feel of Jesus. Why do we ask and wait for his spirit to touch us when we fail to reach out and touch him?

A woman I spoke to who suffered from substance abuse had found herself living a life that she felt ashamed of. Not only was she ashamed, but she was angry. She felt as if life had dealt her a bad hand. She blamed the government for her failure. She complained that as a substance abuser, probation officers did not offer her treatment resources. She complained that even prior to using drugs, people did not reach out to her to offer her assistance to care for her children. To respond, I asked her if she ever considered reaching out for help, assistance, resource information. She sat quietly for about 30 seconds and then answered "no". She said that in all her years of struggling as a young woman and a young mother, she never reached out for help from those whom she felt should have helped her.

So why is it that we don't reach out for what we want? Why is it that we have expectations for others concerning us but do not consider what we can do to have what we want, desire and need?

# Notes

_____  _____

_____

_____

_____

_____

_____

_____

_____

_____

_____

_____

_____

_____

_____

_____

_____

**Window Story**

I love to share this story in trainings and group sessions when I discover that people need help opening their minds.

One day, a beautiful young single woman moved next door to an older married couple.  The wife of the married couple immediately noticed her beauty and began to feel a little jealous.  As the older woman sought reasons for the beautiful lady to appear unattractive to her husband, she spotted the woman hanging up her white laundry.

> *"Oh my, look at those dingy clothes. Does she not know how to wash clothes? That's why she can stay so well-dressed and put together. She probably spends more time getting dressed that she does cleaning. Wait until my husband sees this!"*

So, the wife beckons her husband.  The husband comes running, concerned that there is some trouble.  Confused, the husband slows down his breathing, looks at his wife and tell her that all he sees is the neighbor hanging up her bright white laundry, curious as to what detergent she uses.

By this time, the wife is furious. Her skin turns red and her heart beats fast. Her husband notices her physical reaction and thinks that something must be wrong.  He then walks over to where is wife is and says "Honey, her clothes are white, it's the window you are looking out of that is dirty. When is the last time you cleaned this window?"

Many of us fail to realize that the way we look at things or view things in life causes us to react or respond a certain way. Often, there are times when the consequence of our actions is unfavorable. We must look back to source how our thoughts or perceptions led us to act a certain way.

After realizing that her window was dirty, the woman decides it must be cleaned. She realized her window was filled with negative principles, attitudes and beliefs. Noticing that her neighbor's windows were clean, she inquired how her windows were so clear. The friend replied, "it's simple, I use Windex." After hearing this, she runs to the store to purchase Windex. On the shelf, beside the bottle of Windex she notices another bottle labeled 'Window Cleaner' for a dollar less. The label read, 'compare to the ingredients in Windex.' She decided to take the cheaper route and purchased "Window Cleaner" for $1.99 instead of the Windex brand, which cost $2.99.

How many times have we decided to take the cheaper way out, especially in recovery?

We want to change but hesitate to put in the effort. Many times, I've heard clients say while enrolled in my program, "some of this stuff I believe in and will apply but not all of it."

In the story of the young woman, she comes home to clean her window and notices that it looks worse than before. The window is now foggy and nowhere near clean. Frustrated, she calls her friend to complain. After learning that the woman used the inexpensive window cleaner, her friend let her know that the cleaner was watered down. To properly clean the window, she would have to invest in the more expensive product.

How many times do we lash out on the people who are trying to help us or give us good direction or advise? We want to blame them for our failures knowing that we have not totally been accountable for our own actions.

After understanding her mistake, she went back to the store to ask for a refund. The store clerk informed her that the cleaner could not be refunded because it had already been used.

How many times have we wanted to erase the mistakes we've made or get back the time we have lost? We must get to a point that we are able to accept the things we cannot change. After learning she could not get a refund for the Window Cleaner, she purchased "Windex" which cost her $2.99. She should have initially invested in the right cleaner to avoid the hassle.

I tell this story to those who have been incarcerated multiple times to teach them that is sometimes it takes more than one trip to get what we need to recover.

With the new window cleaner in hand, the woman began to clean her window, noticing it was already looking better. However, there were still white specks on the window. Frustrated as to why the window was still not fully clean, she reached out to her wise grandmother.

Her grandmothers said, "Baby, have you tried old newspaper rather than using paper towels?" Taking the advice into account, she used newspaper and her window immediately looked cleaner.

As she was cleaning the window, she heard a squeaky sound. Now that her window was nice and clean, she could finally be at peace.

A few days later, a wild storm came with gusty winds and pouring rain. In the height of the storm, an old tree created debris that blew onto her beautiful window. The tree in this story represents the things in our lives that we cannot change. We cannot change the mistakes that we have made. We cannot change who our parents are. We cannot change things that have happened to us in the past. She began to cry. Then she realized she had all the tools to clean the window at her disposal.

When you have the right tools, you can shape, structure and control your whole life.

It's simple – the answer lies in changing our perception and reaching our full potential!

When our windows are clean we see things in a different light than the way we did when we looked out of a dirty window. We tend to talk differently because squeaky-clean windows make a squeaky-clean sound. Our language changes. We push people up more than we put them down.

With this new way of viewing the world, we change who we spend time with to only healthy influences. Looking out of a clean window allows us to see debris in our yards. Debris attracts snakes, something we don't want around. Knowing that debris draws snakes, we realize that if we do not clean up our space, we will end up living in fear that a snake is near or in our house!

Who wants to live like that?

We must change who we affiliate with if they cause trouble.

A question that rose in a group session was: was "If I get rid of those people who are unhealthy for me, then how do I replace them with positive people?"

After a lively discussion with the group, we collectively came up with the answer. Looking out of a clean window represents a new way of seeing things. When we look at the world clearly, we open the room for more opportunity. We then tend to reach for our destiny. We start believing that we can accomplish things we once thought were impossible.

Often, we want to change our lives. We do great, but we also want to go back and help our friends, regardless if it puts ourselves in danger. We must remember that such behavior or association can be risky.

# Notes

_____

_____

_____

_____

_____

_____

_____

_____

_____

_____

_____

_____

_____

_____

_____

## Take the Wheel!

When are emotions are high, our reasoning tends to dwindle. To balance our level of thinking and reasoning, we must calm our minds. Trying to think reasonably when angry is one of the biggest challenges.

Think about the last time you made a poor decision in the heat of a moment. Your emotions likely took control. Many people believe that anger is uncontrollable – that is untrue. We all experience anger. It is a natural and healthy emotion.

I have noticed that those who fail to control their anger turn to aggression. When you don't control your anger, you let it steer the car. Anger wants to go south, and you want to go north. If anger is behind the wheel, you will go south. Controlling anger requires that one calms down enough to recognize that anger is present. It requires a person to use their evolved brain and think of ways to manage and control the anger. That's when anger takes the back seat!

# Notes

_____

_____

_____

_____

_____

_____

_____

_____

_____

_____

_____

_____

_____

_____

## Break the fear!

*We should do the thing we say that we cannot do!*

We do not operate under fear for that is restrictive motivation. However, we operate under power, love and a sound mind! We can also refer to that as constructive motivation.

What do I have the power to do?

Anything I put my mind to. One of my recent workshops was about motivation. During the workshop, I challenged clients to use affirmations to build a simulator in their mind. I explained that following a rule just because we are afraid of the consequences means that we are restrictively motivated. The fear of getting caught is not enough to keep us from doing the things we know we shouldn't do. Perhaps someone may wonder why an addict on probation relapses knowing that the consequence would be prison time. Well, to me the answer is simple. I highly doubt that heroin, crack cocaine, marijuana, or any other illegal substance, is afraid of doing time. At therefore, fear alone won't work for someone who is facing prison. To be constructively motivated would mean that there is pay value and or benefit in doing the right thing. Some reward is attached.

When I got home that evening, I thought about my spiritual life. I thought back to when I first learned about the unwelcomed consequences of sin growing up. As I grew spiritually, I began to focus more on the reward of living a sin free life. That focus is what has helped me to create a healthy way of living.

*"For the wages of sin is death, but the gift of God is eternal life in Christ Jesus our Lord (Romans 6:23)".*

Fear has a way of stopping us from achieving our greatest potential. I've met so many people in my professional career that had the potential to do great work that would probably impact the world, but because of fear, they buried their gifts. If you are someone who knows that you have a gift, a talent or an ability, but you do not act because of fear, that one thing that you fear most in doing, is exactly what your calling may be attached to. When I first decided to use my gifts and talents, I realized it would require a boldness. That shy little girl that hid inside of me could not stay with me for long. I had to overcome my fears. Fears of what others would say about me behind my back or fears of failure. I had to literally reconstruct my mind to see the reward of using my gifts. I like to tell others whenever I get the opportunity, "there is always a reward attached to every good and productive thing we do."

**How should you do it?**

Believing that you can and putting forth the work that you are more than able to do.

**Why should you do it?**

 Because you have good intentions and it will have a positive effect.

When discovering your vision, you must look at a few things:

- A. What is it that you want to be or have?
- B. What positive effects will this have on your life?
- C. How will you feel when you have fulfilled your vision?

Try writing a good and constructive affirmation statement using what I have created as the "CAB" formula. Start with C, then A and end with B. Write your statement using present tense words to make your statement true and constructive.

For example:

*I feel motivated because I am writing a book about my life and this has a positive effect on my spiritual growth and professional life.*

# Notes

_____

_____

_____

_____

_____

_____

_____

_____

_____

_____

_____

_____

_____

_____

_____

## Listen

Today, it dawned on me how important it is to listen when having a conversation with someone. What I discovered was that even when someone is speaking but not listening to you talk, it is more so important that you listen to them. This was mindboggling to me because I thought "Why should I even entertain a conversation when I'm the only one who is willing to listen." Then, I had an 'aha' moment.

It would not make any sense to talk if they are not going to listen, now would it? Therefore, listening to them could only be a chance to strengthen the container or atmosphere. Perhaps they choose not to listen because they really have a lot of emotions going on. If their emotions are high, they cannot use proper thinking skills anyway.

# Notes

_____

_____

_____

_____

_____

_____

_____

_____

_____

_____

_____

_____

_____

_____

_____

## It Was NECESSARY!

So many of the things we go through in life are unfortunate. We hurt today over things that may have occurred a decade ago. These things belong in what I have learned to call the circle of concern. They matter to us, but we have no control over them, just like we have no control over what others say about us. We spend too much time in this circle. We tend to get caught up in a downward thinking spiral. Focusing on the things that we cannot change binds up our hands in a sense. We lose focus of the things we do have power over.

Spending too much time in our circle of concern can cause us to feel powerless. Feeling powerless does not motivate us to change the things we can. It's important that we spend more time in our circle of influence. Within that circle are the things we do have power and control over. We have power and control over our thoughts and our behavior.

One way that I decided to deal with remnants of my past that have been hurtful to me was to see those situations as necessary. Just like crops need rain, I realize that I need to see some things as necessary for growth. Surviving those things, overcoming those things, pushing through those things made and shaped me into the very person I am today. I also realized that I am not done growing.

So, things that I may not NECESSARILY like are still NECESSARY! Every now and then, I look back over my life and I am simply amazed with how I have overcome.  Yes, in my mind, IT WAS ALL NECESSARY!

Notes

_____

_____

_____

_____

_____

_____

_____

_____

_____

_____

_____

_____

_____

_____

## Humble Pie

Today, while reading homework assignments I had given to clients about practicing the skill of apologizing, I realized how important humility is for growth. When I thought more about growth and humility, I realized that one's success can easily affect their outlook on life and how they interact and treat other people.

As I meditated more on this, I felt in my spirit that humility is key to handling future successes. There have been times when the words I have chosen to address an issue offended the other person. I didn't want to apologize because those words seemed justified.

I used to think that the people who disrespected others should be able to take disrespect in return. That way of thinking was not working for me. If I wanted to grow and find success, I had to look at that principle and make some changes. I never want to get to the point where I am not humble enough to notice when I make mistakes that hurt or offend people. I realized this morning that the more I am willing to admit my mistakes and apologize while forgiving others who hurt or offend me, I will be able to manage success! Every now and then, we should eat a big slice of humble pie.

# Notes

_____

_____

_____

_____

_____

_____

_____

_____

_____

_____

_____

_____

_____

_____

_____

## Faulty Principles

If the result of your behavior does not meet your needs overtime, then there must be a faulty principle in your belief window.

Some of the principles of my past don't work so well for me now. Times have changed, and I tend to pass my principles down to my children and those who I have impact on. We should understand the impact of our principles.

One principle is that to get respect, one must give it. That simply implies that respect must be earned.

Years ago, that principle worked well for me. However, this very principle may cause unwanted conflict in our lives. For example, if respect is only given when received, then if someone disrespects you, you in return will most likely disrespect them or show them a lack thereof.

With that in mind, I had to create a new principle. A principle to help me in my professional and personal sphere is "everyone deserves respect." When I adopted this new principle, and placed it on my belief window, I began to have better professional relationships which allowed me opportunities that have helped both my personal and professional life. I once heard of a saying, "people might forget what you said, but will tend to remember how you made them feel."

Notes

_____

_____

_____

_____

_____

_____

_____

_____

_____

_____

_____

_____

_____

_____

## Right Now!

There are things that we tend to say that we are waiting until the right time to do or accomplish something. For example, I kept holding off applying for job positions that were good opportunities for me because I felt I had a few things to get right first. Therefore, I missed out on a lot of rewarding experiences. The truth is that there probably won't be many times when we will feel like we are truly ready. Often, we want to wait for a special sign or occasion. However, right now should always be the special occasion.

# Notes

_____

_____

_____

_____

_____

_____

_____

_____

_____

_____

_____

_____

_____

_____

_____

**They Hear It!**

I was attending a conference one week with guest speakers of high caliber and extensive professional experience. While all the speakers were knowledgeable, one young man captured the audience's attention. He had little professional experience and lacked a big title. However, when he began to speak to a room full of professionals, the atmosphere shifted. People were so attentive and moved by his words.

Afterwards, several people approached the young man with questions and statements of appreciation for what he shared with us. This caused me to think about how awesome God is.

Yes, I thought about God at that very moment. There is a reason why God selects the people he does to do certain work. He does not call the qualified however, he qualifies those he calls.

Have you ever wondered why for some reason people hear the voice of certain people?

God creates and identifies these people before they even know just who they are. He'll take the ordinary and change the necessary to make an extraordinary change. People's hearts feel the voice of God when he speaks through people whom he has called and chosen to deliver a message.

# Notes

_____

_____

_____

_____

_____

_____

_____

_____

_____

_____

_____

_____

_____

## Sticky Notes

As I sat at my desk today finishing up some paperwork that had set in my incoming tray for about a week, I realized that it has been over a month since I last added anything to this book. I must admit that this was not the first time I realized how long it had been. My desk is covered in sticky notes of moments I found worthy of being put in a book.

This weekend, a young lady approached me in my dressing room with tears in her eyes. She felt as if she must let me know that she was touched by my singing but most of all she identified my anointing. There was a lot of interesting facts about this woman that caught my attention. She stated that she wanted to take me to Trinidad to sing, which was a great shock for me and my entire band. We were overjoyed with that invitation and more than excited.

Perhaps I was so excited that my mind found it hard to believe that she could or would keep her word. Nevertheless, she approached me again that night in the hallway and handed me a little piece of paper with her name and number on it.

On the bottom of the piece of paper was a note reading, "by the way, have you written the book yet?" There was no way possible she could have known that I was working on a book. She only just met me and all she knew about me was that I was a singer. I had not yet shared with anyone that I had been writing a book. This to me was more than motivation to get back to adding to this book.

I've decided to call the next section of this book **"Sticky Notes."** I want to include those miscellaneous topics that have been collecting through my habit of writing on sticky notes.

## Guard Your Heart

One night, a participant in the group I facilitate stated that she planned to pursue a physical relationship with someone that she has considered a good friend of hers since her incarceration. This was alarming to me, because the participant struggled with maintaining sobriety due to her prior heavy drug use before incarceration. Her drug addiction has had a major impact on her family relationships, especially with her children.

When I voiced my concern that this behavior could possibly cause her to lose focus and not maintain her sobriety, she stated that she did not understand. The subject added that she planned not to fall in love with him but to "have a little fun." One of the most important things that we must remember in life is that most of the time, we don't plan to fall in love or gain strong feelings for people. It just happens. It is important to guard your heart. The issues of the heart can distract a sound mind.

Proverbs chapter 4 verse 23 states, "above all else, guard your heart, for everything you do flows from it."

This does not mean that we cannot afford to love; this simply shows us to take good care of our heart. As a counselor, I struggled with understanding that the heart must first feel and then the mind can change, but how can the heart feel if the mind has not changed.

So why as Christians do we confess something with our mouth first?

It is the heart that must desire something different. The results of our behavior cause us to feel a certain way. Once the heart desires something different, we must start to speak life into what it is that we want to happen differently. After that we must change the way we think about things so that the change we desire can occur. The balance of the heart, the mouth and the mind = a peaceful life.

# Notes

_____

_____

_____

_____

_____

_____

_____

_____

_____

_____

_____

_____

_____

_____

_____

## E+R=L and Earl the Safe Thought!

So, have you ever met that person that has been there and done that? I mean everything, they've done it. Everywhere, they've been. Everything, they've seen. Have you met anyone like that?

This reminds me of a guy I like to call Earl. Earl is that person that's in the audience or in a conversation who has experienced everything. This annoys a lot of people who are around Earl because they don't believe him. There is a possibility that Earl has experienced a lot if not all of the things he says that he has, but people are annoyed because if this is true, he sure does act like a fool. An old fool! You see, experience alone is not the greatest teacher. It is when we reflect on an experience that we learn from it.

Why?

$$\text{E}xperience + \text{R}eflection = \text{L}earning$$

Have you ever looked back over your life and thought about how you handled something? Have you asked yourself "What could I have done better or different?" "Did how I respond work?" "Were people hurt from the way I handled it?" This analytical thinking is learning at its best.

Earl later learned to do this and now is well known in my mind as a man of great wisdom, knowledge and understanding. When I have one of those days when I feel like life has thrown me a curve ball, I use "Earl" as my safe thought. Whenever I find myself starting to complain about how rough my day was, or whenever, a situation occurs, and I am about to respond or react in a way that may get me results I don't like, I think "Where you at Earl?" It works, trust me!

# Notes

_____

_____

_____

_____

_____

_____

_____

_____

_____

_____

_____

_____

_____

_____

_____

_____

**The Answer to Every Problem is Love.**

One day when facilitating a group, I realized that every situation presented by the group members required love for the solution.

What's love got to do with it?

If you think about any problem you have had to solve in life, love was the solution. For example, if people are mistreating you, love will cause you to not retaliate. Love for yourself, love for who you represent, love for the goals you are already on your way to achieving. If you do not retaliate, you will not create a bigger problem. Perhaps you decide to talk it out and understand their feelings even when you don't agree. That's love.

# Notes

_____

_____

_____

_____

_____

_____

_____

_____

_____

_____

_____

_____

_____

_____

_____

## Cognitive Dissonance

I love sharing this theory with everyone I know. I share it with my clients, my coworkers, my friends and my family members every chance I get.

Have you ever decided that you wanted to buy a new car and then afterwards noticed that you started seeing that type of car everywhere? This is because you have locked on to the idea of buying that car and your brain automatically searches for information to support the idea you locked on to. I absolutely love this theory because it has helped me to realize the impact of locking on to different beliefs or principles and their effect.

One day a client posed the question, "what if a person has locked on to two opposite beliefs?" My response was that when there is a battle of two opposite principles or beliefs, the mind starts to experience disharmony. This is not a good feeling and therefore, the mind seeks harmony or peace.

# Notes

_____

_____

_____

_____

_____

_____

_____

_____

_____

_____

_____

_____

_____

_____

_____

**Every setback is a setup for a great comeback!**

There were times when I would find myself complaining and feeling down in the dumps about my life. About three weeks ago, I received what I would call bad news just about every day however, I was determined that I would not complain. During those two weeks, we had a commencement program at my job for those clients who had been enrolled in the program for over four months.

The guest speaker was a man who had spent years in federal prison for drug crimes. During the commencement, it was noted that one of his favorite quotes was "every setback is a setup for a great comeback!" I took this to heart. I've always been one to intentionally not complain. I sometimes felt that my mother was a natural complainer, which annoyed me. Her constant complaining caused me to stress a lot as a child. When I would receive bad news or have what I would call bad experiences, I would fight hard not to get in a complaining mode. I continued to be thankful for not only what I have already been blessed with by God but by what I believed God was about to do in my life.

I recall going to the ATM machine only to find right after payday that most of my money was gone already to bills that were due. Not only that, but someone had also hacked my bank account. I had received so much bad news in a two-week span that I felt I could not take any more. For some reason, money will take me there, or the lack thereof.  So, I got in my car and thought to myself, I have time in this car all by myself to just cry because of the great amount of bad news I had been getting.  I had a 40-minute drive, so I figured I could cry for about 35 minutes however, I could not get in that crying or sad mode, no matter how hard I tried.  My mind wrestled with opposing thoughts and the thoughts of good overtook those thoughts of bad.

I literally experienced the cognitive dissonance theory at its best! That's when, I locked on to the belief, "there must be something so big and great in store for me, which will explain all of the stuff I have been going through."

Notes

_____

_____

_____

_____

_____

_____

_____

_____

_____

_____

_____

_____

_____

_____

_____

## Words Have Power

Move away from the things you don't want and toward the things you do want by affirming your vision. Affirm your vision as though you were already operating in a space where your vision is carried out. Personal affirmation is very powerful, especially when you put what I like to call "spirit behind the word." A wise man once told me that words paint pictures that trigger feelings.

You should never state in your vision what you want to move away from. Never give power to the things that are negative or have a negative effect on your life.

I am reminded of a time I was facilitating a group session and used a personal example of the "old me." While giving a personal example, I thought about a reality TV show reunion I had watched the night before. One of the stars on the show mentioned that an old enemy only came on the show to bring up negative things about her past in attempt to get 15 minutes of fame.

During the class I had an 'aha!' moment and ceased to tell my story. One of the participants asked, "Why did you stop Ms. Macklin?" My response was "I dare not give the old me 15 minutes of fame. She is behind me and I am more amazed with the woman I have become.

Notes

_____

_____

_____

_____

_____

_____

_____

_____

_____

_____

_____

_____

_____

_____

_____

## You Must Attack Your Vision

There is a thought in the Art of War that one way to win is to never back your opponent to the wall where he does not have an escape. If you do, they will have no choice but to come out fighting full force. With that being true, one must look at their visions and goals from an opposite point of view concerning this perspective.

One should back their goal or vision to the wall to a point that it cannot escape them so that their vision will come at them full force. In other words, their vision will be fulfilled.

Sometimes we allow escape routes for our vision and then our vision gets away from us as a result. One way we allow escape routes is when we make our vision statement too vague. For example, someone who has a substance abuse problem can state their vision one of these two ways; "I want to have a healthy lifestyle." This vision statement does not specifically indicate that the person wants to be clean, sober and drug free. Having a statement so vague allows the vision of being drug free to escape. Many people make vague vision statements because they don't feel so bad if they do not fulfill the vision. Instead, one could state, I want to live a sober and healthy life.

.

# Notes

_____

_____

_____

_____

_____

_____

_____

_____

_____

_____

_____

_____

_____

_____

_____

## Birthing your Vision

How long have you been carrying your vision? How long have you been stuck in the same trimester? Have you made plans for the type of birth you will have? Are you prepared for the labor pains? Who is your doctor? How often to you talk with your doctor? Do you follow the instructions of your doctor? What are you feeding your vision? What are the vital signs of your vision? Have you named your vision yet?

These are several questions one must ask themselves when they have a vision of what they want to achieve in life. I think of the vision or goals I set in life in comparison to being pregnant and carrying that vision full term until time for delivery. Do you even know that you are pregnant?

*How long have you been carrying your vision?*

You may have heard some people say for years, "I'm going to do this or I'm going to be this". However, you've been hearing that person say this forever and they seem to not be an inch close to doing or becoming what he or she has set out to do or be. That person would be a prime example of someone staying in the first trimester too long. Imagine finding out you are pregnant at 6 weeks and staying 6 weeks pregnant for years. Imagine morning sickness for years.

*Have you made plans for the type of birth you will have?*

Having a vision or goal requires necessary planning for birth. One must imagine where they will be when they birth their vision or reach their goal. One must also consider who will be present. I've heard wise men and women say that you cannot always take the people you are with now with you when you reach your next destination. Some have said that most people are only in our lives for a season. It is said that everyone in your circle will not be able to elevate with you to your next level. This makes sense to me.

Therefore, it is important that I know where I am going and whom I am going with. Who will I allow to be present with me in the delivery room? Not everyone can stomach you giving birth. This is true. Some people will become so jealous that it will make them sick and they will only begin to become nauseous and regurgitate what is really inside of them. In other words, you'll find out who your real supporters are at some point of carrying your vision. Everyone in your circle may not be happy about your expected due date. So, keeping this in mind will help you to know who to take with you at the next level.

*Are you prepared for the labor pains?*

Sometimes it's in the delivery room when we find out people's real intentions. Sometimes it is not until after we have reached our goal that we find that some of our so-called supporters were really not rooting for us. As long as we were on the same level as they were, they were okay with us. This is one example of labor pains. Have you invested so much into people to the point that them leaving you hurts you so much that you feel life is not fair? You may want to give up, but you can't because you've got a vision to birth. There will be times when you have to push harder than you have ever pushed. The pain and disappointment not only in others but disappointment in ourselves will make us want to throw in the towel and call it quits but we must push harder because we've got a vision to birth. I've heard some people use the word push as an acronym "Pray Until Something Happens." In my mind, praying is pushing.

*Who is your doctor?*

So, I am thinking that after finding out you are pregnant you may want to choose which doctor you would like to have throughout your pregnancy and birthing process. Just like you can choose your physician, you can choose to have Christ as your Savior. Several people have called Jesus Christ their doctor. So, have I. Although I know that just as God has chosen and anointed me to sing, teach, mentor, counsel and lead people; God has also chosen and anointed physicians. So, knowing whose instructions to follow while carrying and birthing your vision or goal is important. There is no better feeling than receiving professional services from someone that knows that they were sent, called, chosen and anointed by God to do so.

You will need some support while carrying your vision and working at reaching your goal. Why not have the support from the best of the best?

# Notes

_____

_____

_____

_____

_____

_____

_____

_____

_____

_____

_____

_____

_____

_____

**Self-Talk**

One day I was facilitating a group about attacking your vision by changing your self-talk. Self-talk to me is a stream of conversation one has with him/herself. It is essentially what we say to ourselves. Even in our talk to others when we affirm things, we must choose our words carefully. Words have power and even life and death has been known to be in the power of the tongue.

So why not speak the things we hope for as if they already exist? Why not breathe life in ourselves using our words?

Words have POWER.

I'll say it again.

Words have POWER.

When we talk about what we want in life, we must choose our words carefully.

# Notes

_____

_____

_____

_____

_____

_____

_____

_____

_____

_____

_____

_____

_____

_____

_____

_____

_____

## Being an Inspiration

I have met so many people during my career who state that they believe their vision or purpose in life is to be a motivator or inspiration for others. Often when I would hear this said, I would feel happy because I solely believe that it is our duty to spread love and inspiration to everyone we encounter.

However, lately I have been feeling slightly confused when I would hear people share that they would like to inspire others. One reason for my confused state is that I have seen and heard many of those people show a lack of inspiration and motivation applied to their own lives.

For example, one young woman who I met at work would share with me that she has low self-esteem and that she constantly has self-defeating thoughts. I asked the young woman how she felt she could inspire, motivate or even encourage others, if she had low self-esteem and was having constant self-defeating thoughts.

Her reply to me was "I am good at inspiring others Ms. Macklin; it's just myself that cannot seem to feel inspired". She began to go on and on saying that she has always been a person that could encourage and inspire others and that others in her community would come to her if they had a problem. Confused, I thought "How can a person pour into someone else's cup if their cup is empty?"

I've always believed that the life we live and the example we model is the best testimony one could ever hear or see.

Notes

_____

_____

_____

_____

_____

_____

_____

_____

_____

_____

_____

_____

_____

_____

## Bad End of the Stick

Have you ever looked at depression as a huge giant in your brain that you fed from the time it was small until the point where it grew so big that it started consuming all your thoughts?

This giant we call depression can be a killer that has never been afraid of anything or anybody.

Why do we choose to feed this giant called "depression"?

What can we do about this giant?

My mother once reminded me that giants do fall! We must first stop feeding the giant so that we can get its "weight" down. Weight in my mind is anything that holds you down mentally, spiritually, emotionally, physically or even financially. This leads to worrying daily. If you don't feed it, it won't grow.

It is important that we feed the right things to ourselves. I personally believe that we all have two energies inside of us and the one that you feed will be the one that will grow.

So, what if we starved our giants? We would no longer think negative thoughts. Instead, starving our giants would encourage what we think is impossible.

A wise woman once said, weak is an individual who does not know his own strength. Strong is an individual who has confidence and feeds themselves positive self-talk.

I had a dream one night that I may have considered a nightmare years ago. Today I consider it a message of power. In this dream there was a giant dragon-like creature that I had to defeat. It was like I was playing a video game, with a bar showing the strength of the dragon in the sky.

As the dragon attempted to take me out, I would throw something at him. As the dragon got frustrated and annoyed, he would say to me, "you can't defeat me, look at how small you are compared to me." This made me feel as if I was fighting a losing battle, but only for a second.

Suddenly, I realized that I had enough power to defeat the dragon. We can defeat any obstacle, attack, weapon etc. if we know the power that is within us. When we feel weak, we fight weak, when we feel strong, we fight strong.

The battles we face in life, even the battles we may have in our own minds, can and will be defeated, if we realize that we have the power and ability to defeat the battle. In other words, it's a fixed fight if we recognize the power and advantage we have.

In this dream, I had the power to defeat the dragon by throwing anything near me at him. The bar in the sky showed the dragon's strength dwindling until he disappeared.

Just as I continued to fight in the dream, you must continue to fight. First you must realize the power that is within you and the resources that are around you. Someone may be reading this and thinking "what power?"

Think about your strengths. Think about the things in you that are positive. Think about the good characteristics and qualities about yourself.

I was having lunch with a young man just 11 years of age and asked him to tell me some good characteristics and qualities about himself. He looked as if he found this difficult to do at first until I rephrased my words and asked him to tell me what he liked about himself. The 11-year-old young man replied, "I love God." After hearing him, I smiled and responded, "awesome and powerful." It seemed as if this 11-year-old boy knew that loving God was something that so many others lacked. I believe that to love God is to know him and to have a relationship with him. Have you ever been bullied when you were in school and you knew that if you told your older sibling or relative, they would defend you and take care of the bully?

Having a close relationship with God to me is a similar situation. Who would worry and stress about defeating the giants in our lives knowing we have that one person that we could definitely call on to defend us. In my dream, the power from God was right in my hand, not thousands of miles or feet away, but right there in the palm of my hand.

We often search for what we need when the answer is with us. Knowing who we are is key. I may not have known everything about the dragon that I defeated, but I came to know who I was and what I had the power to do. Know Thyself!

# Notes

_____

_____

_____

_____

_____

_____

_____

_____

_____

_____

_____

_____

_____

_____

## Keep Your Heart and Your Hands Clean

In one of my sessions, a participant shared that when a person makes fun of or speak negatively about another, it can become messy. Another participant said that she often says things that others find offensive when she means no harm. My response to her was that when this happens, she should make it clear that she meant no harm.

Confused, she inquired further as to why that was necessary. I formed an analogy that not making it clear that you didn't mean harm through words or action is like eating before washing your hands. If your goal and desire is to have a fruitful future that is positive and productive, you must have not only a clean heart but clean hands.

# Notes

_____

_____

_____

_____

_____

_____

_____

_____

_____

_____

_____

_____

_____

_____

_____

**Wisdom Is Knowledge Applied**

Have you ever heard the saying, "If you know better, you would do better?"

What does it profit or benefit us to have all the knowledge in the world if we don't apply the knowledge we already have?

If we know that through a specific action, there will be a negative consequence, why do we continue to choose the same behavior?

We must apply the knowledge learned from past-experiences to propel us forward. This idea of applied knowledge makes me think of the culture of attending trainings/seminars to learn for our jobs. However, when we return to our workplace, we never seem to open the relevant books or materials.

How do we learn to apply what we learn?

We must first practice.

# Notes

_____

_____

_____

_____

_____

_____

_____

_____

_____

_____

_____

_____

_____

_____

_____

## Discovering Your Calling

You may still be wondering what your purpose or calling is. My suggestion is to increase your awareness. To do this, you should meditate daily until your awareness is increased. There will come a time when you will begin to hear from God during your prayer and meditation, exactly what he is trying to say to you. The more time you spend talking with God and thinking about him, the more you will discover. I've learned to make it my business to take time with God before leaving my home in the morning and before going to bed at night. If you're looking to discover your purpose, simply start there and take notes.

# Notes

_____

_____

_____

_____

_____

_____

_____

_____

_____

_____

_____

_____

_____

_____

_____

## Conclusion

It is a wonderful feeling to have accepted the call in my life. To know my purpose gives me immense pleasure in my work. I am overjoyed to know that I have a purposeful life.

Will I discover other gifts, talents and abilities of mine?

I'm certain I will. With the power within me, I will accept every opportunity to use those gifts, talents and abilities. Most importantly, I have learned that my calling is to use my gifts to intercede and I am so excited about the work that has begun in me.

> *"I am sure of this, that he who began a good work in you will bring it to completion at the day of Jesus Christ (Philippians 1:6)."*

Just to be able to intercede on someone's behalf is an honor. I remember when I realized that my true calling was to be an intercessor. I began to study about such a calling. I also began to seek instruction and guidance from God. My heart has always been able to pick up the need to intervene, to step in and carry some of the load regardless if I knew the person. People may question if I ever get tired. My response is no. There is some source of energy that ignites in me to provide the incredible power of *connection*. As you read this, I would like you to know that I have already considered you. I have already meditated on how you reading this book can influence your life. Yes, **YOUR** life!

It is my desire and request that your life is never the same but more positive, hopeful, fruitful and successful because you have taken the time to read about my call, my answer and my experience. *Live on purpose!*